The Cambridge
Library of Ornamental Art

Renaissance Ornament

—The Cambridge—
Library of Ornamental Art

RENAISSANCE ORNAMENT

from the 15th to the 17th century

Wordsworth Editions

This edition published 1991 by Wordsworth Editions Ltd,
8b East Street, Ware, Hertfordshire.

Copyright © Wordsworth Editions Ltd 1991.

ISBN 1-85326-956-5

Printed and bound in Hong Kong by South China Printing Co.

Acknowledgements

The illustrations in this book are reproduced by kind permission of the Syndics of the Cambridge University Library. They are taken from *The Grammar of Ornament* by Owen Jones, *Coloured Ornament* by Alexander Speltz, *The Treasury of Ornament* by Heinrich Dolmetsch, and *Arts of the Middle Ages and Renaissance* by Paul Lacroix.

The publishers would like to thank the many staff at the Cambridge University Library who helped in the publication of this book, especially David Hall, Under Librarian (Administration), Nigel Hancock, Head of Reader Services, and Gerry Bye, Head of Photographic Services and his staff.

List of Plates

1. Majolica ware 15th-17th centuries. Specimens of Hispano-Arabic, French and Italian earthenware preserved in the Victoria and Albert Museum, London.

2. French Stoneware. Stoneware from Oiron was much prized from the sixteenth century onwards.

3. Italian embroidery and carpet weaving. 1: Embroidery on an ecclesiastical mantle. 2: Embroidered velvet cover. 3: Embroidered border of a chasuble. 4: Silk appliqué-work for a chasuble. 5: Relief embroidery in gold on silk from a chasuble. 6,7: Silk embroideries in appliqué on a damask ground. 8-10: Carpet borders from an Italian picture.

4. Italian precious metal painting and enamel. 1: Altar crown. 2: Lapis lazuli vase. 3: Gold enamelled crystal cup. 4,5: Cellini pendants. 6-8: Pendants, 9,10: Handles. 11,12: Masks. 13,14: Water jug. 15-19: Borders on various vessels.

5. Italian illumination, weaving and marble mosaic. 1-6: Paintings from manuscripts. 7: Velvet stuff. 8: Silk stuff border. 9: Marble mosaic.

6. Italian pottery painting. 1: Madonna relief. 2: Florentine vestry-fountain. 3-13: Dishes from Faenza. 14-19: Dishes from Chaffagiolo. 20: Dishes from Gubbio. 21-27: Dishes from Urbino. 28,29: Dish from Pesaro.

7. French enamel on metal, pottery painting and metal mosaic. 1-10: Decorations on Limoges vessels. 11,12: Faience gable ends. 13-18: Decorations on faience vessels by Bernard Palissy. 19,20: Faience plate borders. 21: Little boule chest.

8. Sgraffiti, wood-mosaic, marble and bas reliefs. 1-5: Roman sgraffiti. 7: Inlaid marble, Siena. 8,11: Italian inlaid marble. 12,15: Italian bas reliefs.

9. Gobelin tapestries. 1-3: Borders on a tapestry carpet, 1665-72, after Le Brun. 4-6: Border on a tapestry, 1670-80, after Coypel. 7: Border from a 16th-century tapestry.

10. Italian arabesques. Painted in fresco on a white ground, in the Palazzo Ducale, Mantua.

11. German ceiling and wall painting, wood mosaic and embroidery. 1: Wall painting from the bathrooms of the Fugger house in Augsburg. 2-5: Wall and ceiling paintings from the Knights' Hall of the Trausnitz at Landshut. 6: Wood inlaid chest. 7: Embroidered linen border.

12. German stained glass painting. Glass paintings from the dome of the rich chapel in the royal residence at Munich.

13. German ornamented book-covers. 1: Silver-edged book-cover. 2-36: Decoration on pigskin bindings.

14. French decoration in the Hotel Cluny. 1-32: 15th-17th century faience. 33: 17th-century carved wood panel. 34-38: Enamelled earthenware. 39-42: Silk embroidery on velvet.

15. Bas reliefs. 1,2: Genoa. 3: Ghiberti Gate, Baptistry, Florence.
    4,5,8,9,11: Genoa. 6: Venice. 7: S. Giovanni e Paolo, Venice.
    8: Hotel Bertheroude, Rouen.

16. 16th-century typography. Embellishments from France and
    Italy selected from the Aldines, the Giuntas, the Stephans
    and others.

17. German book ornamentation: textile figures.
    1,3,7,10: Sixteenth-century galloons from linen wefts.
    2: Embroidery. 4,6,8,9: Tissues from the sixteenth century.

18. French ceiling painting. 1-4: Castle at Blois, Francois I.
    5-8: Castle at Videville, Louis XIII.

19. Italian silk & velvet. 1,3,8: North Italian silk. 4,5,9: Venetian
    velvet and brocade. 6,7: Genoese velvet.

20. German embroidery & weaving. 1: Table cover. 2: Bavarian
    linen. 3: Embroidered border from a carpet. 4: Carpet
    embroidered on cloth. 5: Curtain border. 6: Border of a
    leather pouch. 7: Woven pattern in Weingarten Church.

21. Faience & majolica ware. 1-21: 15th-17th century French
    faience columns. 22,23: 16th-century German pottery *en grès*
    (stoneware) with painted glaze. 24-34: French, Spanish and
    Italian earthenware.

22. French block printing & embroidery. 1,2,4: 17th-century
    relief printing. 3: 17th-century flat printing. 5: 16th-century
    border on an embroidered carpet.

23. Italian majolica tiles. 1-3: 15th-century tiles from Siena &
    Amalfi. 4: Tiles from Nilo S. Matteo and Via Luccole, Genoa.

24. French wood & stone carving, 15th & 16th century.

25. Elizabethan decoration. 1,15,18: Diapers, Burton Agnes.
    2: Diaper, Trinity College, Cambridge. 3,9: Westminster
    Abbey. 4: Diaper, Enfield. 5: Diaper, Tottenham. 6,8: Diapers,
    Trinity College Cambridge, James I. 7: Needlework tapestry.
    10: Chair damask, Knowle. 11,13: Appliqué needlework.
    12,14,16,17: Elizabethan and Jacobean dress patterns.

26. French painted wood ceilings. 1,2,5: Chateau de Videville,
    Louis XIII. 3: Assizes, Dijon. 4: Chateau d'Auet, Henri II.

27. Late Renaissance. Italian painted ceilings.

28. Carpet painting. Painted carpet-patterns in the castle at Blois
    from the time of Francois I.

29. French decoration. 1: Painted frieze. 2: Carved wood panel.
    3,4: Carved and painted girder panels. 5: Carved and painted
    ceiling panel. 6,7: Book-covers. 8: Painted wall panel.
    9: Painted wall frieze. 10,11: Painted stucco frieze. 12: Border
    of a Gobelin.

30,31. A series of arabesques, painted in fresco by various artists from
    designs by Raphael, in the central open arcade of the Vatican.

32. Italian inlaid marble. 1,2,6,7: Tarsia from Padua. 3: Tarsia
    from Certosa near Padua. 4: Tarsia from S. Domenico,
    Messina. 5: Tarsia in the Museo Pio Clementino, Rome.

33. German plasterwork. From the Knights' Hall of the castle of
    Heiligenberg.

34. German typographic ornament. 1: Title frame by Hopfer.
    2: Durer initials. 3: Frieze by Aldengrave. 4: Holbein initial.
    5: Marginal decoration from the prayer-book of the Emperor
    Charles V by Durer. 6: Beham frieze. 7-11,13: Initials.
    12: Frieze. 14: Headpiece by Theodor de Bry. 15: Tailpiece
    by von Bemmel.

35. Italian tarsia. 1,7: S. Maria Novella, Florence. 2,3,5: S. Maria
    in Organo, Verona. 4: Certosa, near Pavia. 6: S. Marco,
    Venice.

36. Italian ceiling & wall painting. 1: Tympanum from the Sala Ducale, Vatican. 2-5: Details from the Loggie di Raffaelle, Vatican. 6-8: Severey and plafond borders in the Villa di Papa Giulio, Rome. 9: Pilaster panels, S. Maria Aracelli, Rome. 10: From the cloister of the monastery of S. Maria sopra Minerva, Rome.

37. Arabesques designed by Guilio Romano painted in fresco in the Palazzo del Te, Mantua.

38. French typographic ornament. 1,2: Initials by Tory. 3: Initial by Garamond. 4,5: Cartouche and initial by Goujon. 6-8: Initials from Saloman Bernard's school. 9-11: Borders by Petit Bernard. 12: Initial by Tornesius. 13: Initial from the time of Henri IV, 16th century. 14: Initial from the time of Louis XIII, 17th century. 15: Louis XIII tailpiece.

39. French ornamental designs. 1-8: Enamel. 9: Background to a picture. 10,11: Enamels on gold ground. 12: Silver inlay. 13-17: Designs from objects in the Hotel Cluny. 18-24: Enamels. 25: Ebony. 26: Inlay. 27,28: Pottery. 29: Champlevé enamel. 30: Painted ornaments. 31: Detail from the armour of Henri III. 32: Metal plate. 33-35: Metal work. 36: Armour of Francois II. 37-39: Repoussé ornaments. 40,41: Champlevé enamel. 42-44: Goldsmiths' work in the Louvre. 45,46: Enamel picture. 47: Ornament in copper. 48: Ivory inlay. 49: Painted ornament. 50-53: Champlevé enamel. 54-56: Accessories to picture. 57-61: Champlevé enamel.

40. German embroidery, leather, tapestry and goldsmiths' work. 1: Embroidery. 2: Embroidered chasuble. 3: Border of stamped leather hangings. 4,5: Decorations on a silver drinking cup.

41. German ceiling and wall paintings from the Golden Hall at Urach. 1: Spandril. 2: Window panel. 3,4: Column decorations. 5: Parapet decoration. 6,7: Sections of friezes. 8-11: Ceiling beams. 12: Wooden hood moulding.

42. Italian arabesques. Painted on fresco on a partially-coloured ground, Palazzo Ducale Mantua.

43. Spanish helmets. Elaborately chased and ornamented armour from the sixteenth century.

44. Oiron faience. A sixteenth-century Henri II biberon showing the rich and elegant interlacing characteristic of the style.

45. German sixteenth-century wall painting. 1-8: Portions of painted frescoes in the church at Freudenstadt. 9: Door-panel by Wendel-Dieterlein, painter at Strasbourg, 1598.

46. Painted stucco. 1: Wall decoration in the Palazzo Andrea Doria. 2,3: Door frames in the Ducal Palace, Urbino.

47. Italian majolica. Fifteenth and sixteenth century Italian majolica patterns. 9 is a rare dish with three sections and centrepiece showing an antique sacrifice.

48. Venetian book-ornamentation. The late fifteenth and early sixteenth centuries saw a typographical flowering in the Venetian republic, and encompassed such notables as Alessandro Paganini, Aldus Manutius and Bernardino de Novara.

Renaissance Ornament

THE RENAISSANCE is generally regarded as that rich period of development in European civilization that marked the transition from the Middle Ages to modern times. In Italy, the Renaissance had emerged by the fourteenth century and reached its height in the fifteenth and sixteenth; elsewhere in Europe it may be dated from the fifteenth to the mid-seventeenth centuries. In outlook, the Renaissance brought new importance to individual expression, self-confidence and worldly experience. Culturally, it was a period of brilliant accomplishments in scholarship, literature, science and the arts.

From the second half of the thirteenth century it is possible to detect the break with medieval methods of depicting the visible world. The Florentine painter and architect Giotto di Bondone (c1266-1337) was one of the first of those who began painting the human form in a new and more realistic fashion, and he established the representation of nature and space in ways that had not previously been attempted successfully. In architecture, too, there were Brunelleschi (1377-1446) and Alberti (1404-72), who each visited Rome to study the ruins so that they might incorporate the architectural principles of classical antiquity into their own work. Developments in the fine arts, architecture, music and literature are usually echoed by changes in the crafts and decorative professions. The more strictly ornamental painting of the Renaissance may be said to have developed most rapidly during the fifteenth century. In general, it was an adaptation of antique forms, but using a free treatment, and this applied particularly to the most common motifs, especially in botanical forms. Almost everywhere, there are delicate, beautifully curved branches in symmetrical or at least regular arrangement, in which the classical acanthus leaf plays a principal part. Vine, laurel, ivy and fruits are all in evidence, sometimes natural, sometimes stylized, but this foliage is enlivened by a rich variation of animals, fantastical beings and human figures as well as symbolical subjects, arms, masks, emblems, vases and candelabra. In the later Renaissance, an important part of the decoration was of coats of arms and escutcheons, the latter usually as shields or cartouches.

Stained or painted glass declined in importance in accordance with the classical tradition that was influencing architecture. The major exception was in northern Europe where guild-rooms, town halls, the castles of the nobility, colleges and houses of prominent citizens frequently contained glass, beautifully painted with symbolical or historical representations or coats of arms. With the acquisition of advanced techniques, glass painters were able to execute great figural compositions which do not otherwise lend themselves so readily to the medium. Throughout most of the continent, however, there was less emphasis on such attention to window glass, and at the same time wall surfaces ceased to be so elaborately painted, being covered instead with decorated cloths to add comfort and an element of insulation to meeting-halls and bed-chambers. From the sixteenth century onwards wall carpets found favour in the houses of the wealthy, and hangings of wool woven in the Netherlands and embellished with figural representations were sold all over the world, superseding silk and linen tapestry. Later on, in France under Louis XIV, a manufactory of tapestry was established by the Gobelin brothers, after whose tapestries all fabrics of this kind came to be named.

Other domestic arts underwent astonishing developments during the Renaissance, and ceramics played a leading part. In the middle of the fifteenth century, Hispano-Moresque wares became very popular in Italy, and since they were imported via Majorca, they became known as *majolica*. It has been said of majolica that it is as representative of the Renaissance as stained glass is of the Gothic world, or carpet weaving of the Islamic. Italian majolica manufacturers grew and flourished in Tuscany, Faenza, Urbino and Venice, and these and other centres saw the heyday of the medium: vessels were nobly proportioned and gaily painted with subjects that varied from the heraldic and completely formal to commemorative portraiture and classical and biblical stories. High temperature colours and lustre glazes further enriched this beautiful workmanship. In the sixteenth century, potters from Faenza carried the art into France, Spain and the Low Countries, and the name of the ware changed from majolica into *faience*. Though faience is basically synonymous with majolica, by custom the former word is applied to objects made in the seventeenth century or later.

A brief but brilliant school of French faience grew up at Oiron between 1529 and 1568 under the artistic control of Helene de Hougest and her husband Artus Gouffier. Only a few examples of this work have survived. They have a delicate and harmonious design that seems to have been inspired more by the goldsmith's art than by architecture. They exhibit pure forms and an ivory tint, and most of the surviving pieces are parts of a dinner service designed for Henri II and Diane de Poitiers.

Book ornamentation in both printing and binding is another art that marks the Renaissance. The development of moveable type by Johann Gutenberg in Mainz was confined chiefly to black-letter or Gothic typography, and this style was adhered to for theological and juridical works. However, by the 1460s Italian printers were experimenting with Renaissance characters, and by the 1570s the blank spaces which had previously been illuminated by hand in imitation of earlier manuscripts were being ornamented with splendid initials, borders and vignettes, and the whole process of book production became a rich art-form which now embraced the secular and scientific as well as the religious and classical, to which it had largely been restricted in earlier times.

The great flowering of all artistic and scientific thought which we call the European Renaissance, and which extended across the whole landscape of cultural life from music to architecture and from poetry to philosophical ideas, had an enormous impact upon the development of the Western mind and our feelings about the world in which we live. While the great progress and advantages brought about by this important period in our history are evident and much-vaunted, it must be remembered that much, too, was lost. The rise of Rationalism and the Individual was to bring with it self-confidence, yes, but also self-confidence's shadow, Doubt; and the more scientific and 'objective' view of the natural world was accompanied by a sense of distance and separation, the loss of the more symbiotic relationship with nature and the feeling of wholeness that had been the world-view of Western man until the Middle Ages. But it was a development that was as inevitable and necessary as a child's leaving home and finding its own sense of Selfhood: an important stage in our social, cultural and political growth. It is evident from the world about us now, however, that the separation and distance have perhaps stretched too far, and, like the Prodigal Son, we must somehow bring about a reconciliation and return. At such an important juncture in the history of mankind as we stand at now, a renewed study of both Renaissance and Medieval art and thought can only be beneficial for us all.

Plate 1

Plate 2

Plate 3

Plate 4

Plate 5

Plate 6

Plate 7

K. Schaupert gez.

Plate 8

Plate 9

Plate 10

Plate 11

Plate 12

Plate 13

Plate 14

TAFEL LXXV

PL. LXXV

Plate 15

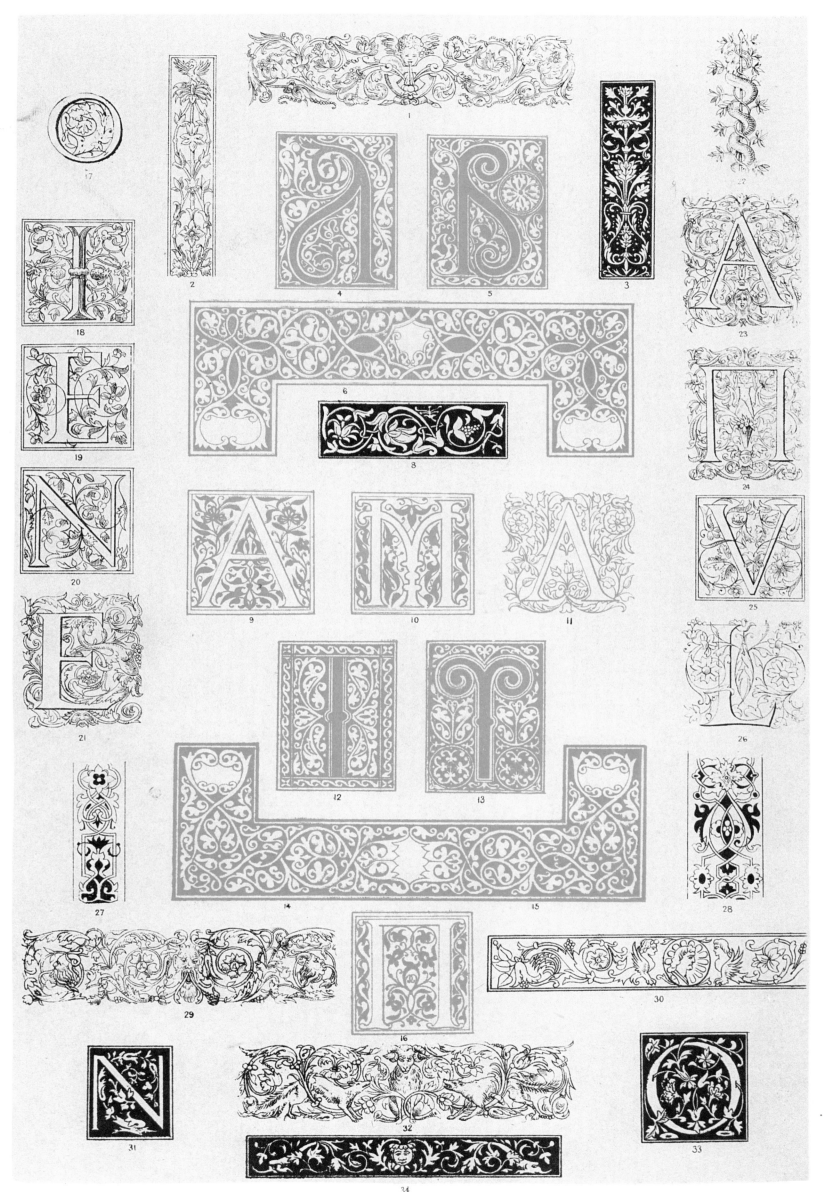

Plate 16

Plate 17

Plate 18

1.

2.

3.

4.

5.

6.

7.

8.

9.

Plate 19

Plate 20

Plate 21

Plate 22

Plate 23

Plate 24

Plate 25

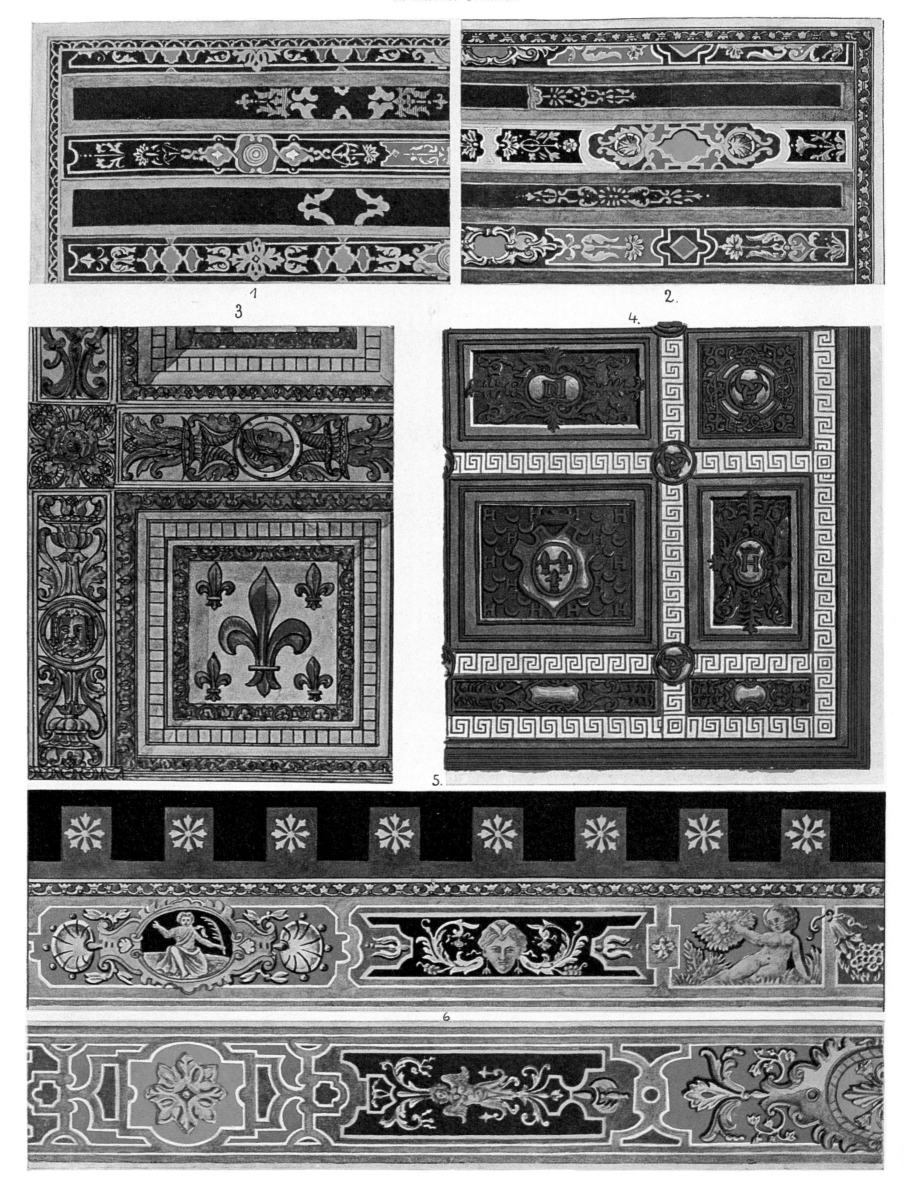

Plate 26

Plate 27

Plate 28

Plate 29

Plate 30

Plate 31

Plate 32

Plate 33

Plate 34

Plate 35

Plate 36

Plate 37

MORS · IN ME · IN ME VITA

Plate 38

Plate 39

Plate 40

Plate 41

Plate 42

Plate 43

Plate 44

Plate 45

Plate 46

Plate 47

Plate 48